the art of
Mindful
Living

how to slow down
and live mindfully

An Hachette UK Company
www.hachette.co.uk

First published in Great Britain in 2021 by Pyramid,
an imprint of Octopus Publishing Group Ltd.
Carmelite House
50 Victoria Embankment
London, EC4Y 0DZ
www.octopusbooks.co.uk

Distributed in the US by
Hachette Book Group
1290 Avenue of the Americas
4th and 5th Floors
New York, NY 10104

Distributed in Canada by
Canadian Manda Group
664 Annette St.
Toronto, Ontario, Canada M6S 2C8

ISBN: 978-0-7537-3469-8

A CIP catalogue record for this book is available from the British Library

Printed and bound in China

10 9 8 7 6 5 4 3 2

Publisher: Lucy Pessell
Designer: Hannah Coughlin
Junior Editor: Sarah Kennedy
Editorial Assistant: Emily Martin
Production Controllers: Nic Jones and Lucy Carter

the art of
Mindful
Living

how to slow down
and live mindfully

introduction

Mindfulness is a state of mind achieved by focusing one's awareness on the present moment, while calmly acknowledging and accepting one's feelings, thoughts, and bodily sensations. In this book you will find a collection of tips for practicing mindfulness throughout your day-to-day life, accompanied by quotes to help engage and inspire you.

Adopting a mindful lifestyle doesn't have to mean taking hours out of your day to meditate. In fact, every situation you find yourself in presents an opportunity to practise mindfulness: waiting at the bus stop, queuing in a shop, even performing household chores ...

Just taking a few minutes each day to ground yourself in the present moment can be hugely beneficial to both your physical and mental well-being. Increasingly, research is suggesting that mindfulness can lower stress levels, blood pressure, improve your quality of sleep and so much more. Developing the habit of daily mindfulness will likely improve your overall quality of life and your levels of happiness, as well as bringing a sense of inner peace.

Mindfulness can feel counterintuitive to our usual way. We are busy, so we rush. We have too much to do, so we multitask. Conversely, to be mindful is to slow down and focus on one task at a time. You will actually improve your productivity if you can manage to do this and you will certainly live your life with a greater sense of calm.

To be mindful is to learn how to fully appreciate life's little pleasures and the most precious of moments that, all too often, pass by unnoticed when the mind is distracted. Don't let another year slip through your fingers in the blink of an eye. Use this book as your guide, inspiration and motivation to embrace everyday mindful living.

how to use this book

As you work your way through this book, you may find that some tips and exercises work better for you than others – and that's okay. The journey to a mindful life is completely different for everyone, so it's important to do what feels right for you.

It is also entirely up to you on what order you decide to work through the book. You may wish to read it from start to finish, or you may prefer to dip in and out of it as you need. You may find it helpful to bookmark the tips that work well for you, so that you can come back to them at a later time.

Lastly, don't become frustrated if the tips in this book don't work for you straight away. Mindfulness requires practice and cannot be mastered overnight. Take your time, and practice it when you can in small increments. If you become tired or unfocused, take a break or stop and carry on the following day. You will find this a far more rewarding experience on your journey to mindfulness.

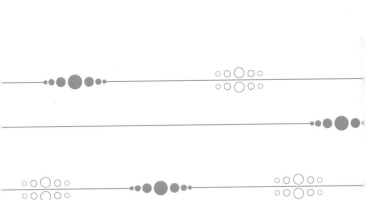

the body scan

If you want to conquer the anxiety of life, live in the moment,
live in the breath.

Amit Ray, spiritual master

The body scan meditation is a great place to start your
mindfulness journey.

Make yourself comfortable, lying on your back on the
floor or on your bed. Allow your eyes to close gently. Take
a few moments to get in touch with the movement of your
breath and the sensations in your body. When you are
ready, begin by focusing your attention on the tips of your
toes and then move up the body slowly, focusing on each
body part as you go; the ball and heel of the foot. The sides
and upper part of the foot. The ankle ... As you breathe in,
imagine the breath going down your body and into your
toes. As you breathe out, imagine the breath going back
up your body and out of your nose. Repeat this process of
gentle awareness of each body part and sensation until you
reach the top of your head.

mindful communication

Respond; don't react. Listen; don't talk. Think; don't assume.

Raji Lukkoor, author

Today, practise bringing your mindful attention to your interactions with others. Focus on making eye contact with the people you communicate with, on really seeing them.

We have all become far too reliant on using social media to stay in touch with our friends and family. And when we're pressed for time, it's all too easy to just send a quick text message to say hello. But over time, communicating in this way can feel unfulfilling and hollow. This is why it's so important to take time to practise mindful meditation.

create a "to-be" list

My goal today is to live in a state of grace and lightness.
I will not invite struggle or drama. I will say yes more
and smile often.

Kimberley Blaine, family therapist

This is an alternative to a to-do list. Halfway through the
day, pause and take a minute to ask, "How am I being right
now?" Curt or understanding? Defensive or open-minded?
Dismissive or kind? Turn your "to-be" list into a goal and
try to maintain it on a discreet post-it on your desk, or
wherever you are likely to see it, to keep your intentions
in check.

do nothing

Allow yourself to rest. Your soul speaks to you in the quiet
moments in between your thoughts.

Anonymous

Even if it's just for five minutes, sit for that five minutes
and do ... nothing. Sit silently in a comfortable chair or in
a sunny spot outside, if possible without mobile phones
or other distractions near you. Become still. Bring your
full awareness into the present moment. All that exists
for you is the here and now. You may be amazed at how
pleasurable and satisfying it is just to "be", and how much
taking just five minutes from your day will give back to
your life as a whole.

When you first try to sit still and do nothing, you may
find that you become easily distracted, and that anxious
or stressed thoughts might start to creep their way in. But
with practice over time, you will find it gets easier to be
completely still and to bring your mind to rest.

mindful walking

Walk as if you are kissing the Earth with your feet.

Thích Nhất Hạnh, peace activist

Walking can give you a chance to spend time being mindful without taking any extra time out of your day. Wherever you are walking to or from today, turn it into a meditative exercise. Walk slowly, paying attention to the sensations on the soles of your feet. Notice as each part of the sole, from heel to toe, touches the ground. Lifting, moving, placing. Lifting, moving, placing. Notice how the body moves as you walk. Walk with awareness. One step at a time. Notice any thoughts that arise and let them be.

You may find it beneficial to find a quiet place to practise mindful walking. Rather than walking along a busy road, try and find a quiet, open space where you are less likely to be distracted.

take five

Mindfulness [...] is being open to or receiving the present moment, pleasant or unpleasant, just as it is, without either clinging to it or rejecting it.

Sylvia Boorstein, author and psychotherapist

Every now and then throughout the day, challenge yourself to find five things that are part of your present experience.

First notice five things that you can see with your eyes. They don't necessarily have to be interesting; it might just be a table, the carpet or a cup in front of you. The aim is simply to bring your full awareness to your experience now in the present moment.

Then notice five things you can hear. Keep listening until you've distinguished five different sounds.

Then notice five things you can feel with your body. These might be the material of your clothes, a slight breeze or even tension in your neck.

be here now

Life can be found only in the present moment. The
past is gone, the future is not yet here, and if we do not
go back to ourselves in the present moment, we cannot be
in touch with life.

Thích Nhất Hạnh, peace activist

This great piece of advice comes from the well-known
spiritual teacher, Ram Dass:

We should ask ourselves: Where am I?

Answer: Here.

Then ask ourselves: What time is it?

Answer: Now.

Keep repeating until you really feel grounded in the
present moment.

get up early to watch the sunrise

Thoughts are slow and deep and golden in the morning.

John Steinbeck, author

The thought of getting up at the crack of dawn may be far from relaxing for many of us, but if you make the effort to do this you will feel revived and refreshed throughout the day as well as carrying a stronger sense of awareness and inner peace. Contemplate the sunrise, absorb the beauty of its colours, notice every aspect of the changing light, embrace the start of a new day. Whatever tasks lie in the day ahead, for these moments let your thoughts be still.

mindful tea meditation

Drink your tea slowly and reverently, as if it is the axis on
which the world earth revolves – slowly, evenly, without
rushing towards the future; live the actual moment. Only this
moment is life.

Thích Nhất Hạnh, peace activist

Wrap both your hands around your mug of tea (or other
warm beverage). Focus on the warmth radiating through
the mug into your hands and breathe deeply. Notice how
comforting it is to hold this warm mug between your
hands – soothing and relaxing. Really pay attention and
breathe deeply for a couple of minutes. Then take your first
sip and savour the taste. Focus your mind on the taste. Be
aware of how much you enjoy this drink. How the liquid
flows over your tongue and down your throat, leaving this
16   wonderful taste that you so appreciate in your mouth.

label your worries

We spend precious hours fearing the inevitable. It would be
wise to use that time adoring our families, cherishing our
friends and living our lives.

Maya Angelou, author

When you find yourself worrying about something today,
consciously stop and label what you are doing as "just
worrying." Then bring your attention back to your breath
or simply change the subject of your thinking. Every time
you catch yourself worrying, just label it again and change
the subject.

Labelling your worries as they arise in this way provides
a sense of separation from your thoughts and will help
you to put them into perspective. You may even find it
helps to write your worries down in a notebook and then
put it away on a shelf or in a cupboard. As you do so, feel
yourself acknowledging your worry, getting it out of your
system by writing it down, and putting it out of your mind
by leaving it on the shelf.

a space for you

Sometimes you need to take a break from everyone and spend time alone, to experience, appreciate and love yourself.

Robert Tew, motivational speaker

Today, create a space in your house that is just for you. A calm haven from both the outside world and the comings and goings of the rest of your household. Choose a few of your favourite items – maybe paintings or photographs that make you feel calm or happy – to decorate the space. Maybe a comfortable chair or cushion to sit on, a scented candle, your favourite book. Whatever makes it feel calm, inviting and just for you.

It's so important to have a space that is just for you, that serves as a retreat for when you need some time alone to be with your thoughts. In addition to the above, make sure you pay attention to colours and lighting, as these can have a big impact on your mood and state of mind.

make everyday magical

I don't have to chase extraordinary moments to find happiness. It's right in front of me if I'm paying attention and practising gratitude.

Brené Brown, lecturer and author

Find a bit of magic in your day. It may be the sound of the rain, the laughter of a loved one, the clouds in the sky or a quiet moment alone. Whatever it is – and however small – make the magic moment count. Acknowledge it, appreciate it, embrace it.

It is worth remembering that magic can be found in even the most seemingly mundane parts of life. For example, perhaps you're having to hang out your laundry to dry. Rather than seeing it as just another chore that needs completing, find joy in the feeling and smell of freshly washed clothes, ready for when you next plan on wearing them.

19

declutter

Clutter stops the flow of positive energy in your space and ultimately in your life.

Jayme Barret, feng shui consultant

Set some time aside today to declutter an area of your home or workspace. Although it may seem overwhelming at first, doing this can actually be as peaceful as a meditation. Clutter is a way of holding on to the past, or fearing the future. Letting go of clutter is a way to live more mindfully and in the present.

You may sometimes find it hard to get rid of items that are cluttering up your space. You may find yourself thinking "what if I want to wear this item again?" or "what if this item comes in handy in the future?" even when, deep down, you know you no longer want the item. Rather than throwing it away, why not donate it to charity or hand it down to a family member or friend? That way you know the item will be put to good use rather than sitting in the back of your cupboard or being thrown straight in the bin.

commute mindfully

Rivers know this: there is no hurry. We shall get there some day.

A.A. Milne, author

Instead of wishing the journey away, embrace the time that it has afforded you to sit and be. Be mindful of your emotions as they rise and fall, come and go. Recognize the frustration, anger, impatience that may arise, but rather than thinking about them, judging them, or analysing them, simply acknowledge them.

If you find your commute is particularly stressful, why not put together a playlist of music that helps you to feel calm so that you can fully engage with your thoughts and keep stress and anxiety at bay.

21

laugh

The most wasted of all days is one without laughter.

Nicolas Chamfort, writer

Laughing brings us into the present moment in a mindful way and is a great stress reliever. Try sticking on a funny film, read a funny book or call an old friend and reminisce about good times.

Not only does laughter improve your mood in the short term, it also has many physical benefits. Along with enhancing your intake of oxygen, laughter also stimulates your heart, lungs and muscles, and increases the endorphins that are released by your brain.

There may of course be times when you really don't feel like laughing. During these times, try and force a laugh – even if it feels a bit strange. Afterwards, ask yourself if you feel a little different. Do you feel a little lighter? Have your muscles become slightly looser?

stolen moments

Your mind is your instrument. Learn to be its master
and not its slave.

Remez Sasson, author

The concept of wasted time does not exist for a mindful person. Every spare moment can be used for meditation. Feeling irritated while queuing at the post office? Meditate on irritation. Sitting anxiously in the doctor's waiting room? Meditate on your anxiety. Bored waiting at the bus stop? Meditate on boredom. Try to stay alert and aware throughout the day. Be mindful of exactly what is taking place right now. Today, use every spare second to be mindful. Use all the moments you can.

When you start to make this a regular habit, you'll notice that time almost starts to feel as if it's slowing down. If you make the most of every single part of your day, it will help you to sleep easy at night, with a sense of fulfilment and achievement – even if, on the surface, your day may not have been particularly exciting or productive.

monotask

The only true thing is what's in front of you right now.

R. Amona Ausubel, author

Do one thing at a time. There is a growing body of evidence that suggests multitasking makes us less efficient, less effective, more stressed and more likely to make mistakes. Maintaining focus and interest on one task at a time is not easy, but start practising today.

For example, if you are at work and you are faced with having to complete a big task that requires a lot of concentration and attention to detail, turn your emails off and put your phone on silent (or better yet, switch if off!). You will find you are much more productive without the constant stream of notifications to distract you. If you are worried about your colleagues not being able to get hold of you, why not set an out-of-office that alerts them to the fact that you are currently putting time aside to concentrate on a separate task, and will be back in touch with them as soon as possible?

pebble in your pocket

The mind is everything. What we think, we become.

Buddha

Such a simple thing, and yet something that Zen masters the world over do, is to keep a pebble in a pocket. Do this and each time you put your hand in your pocket, hold the pebble gently and let it serve as a reminder to pause, smile and calmly breathe in and out.

For a special and more meaningful touch, you can use a smooth tumbled crystal in place of a pebble. Different crystals have different healing properties, so do your research and pick one that feels right for you. For example, amethyst can be good for reducing anxiety, and moonstone is known for its mellowing properties.

exercise mindfully

When it comes to health and wellbeing, regular exercise is about as close to a magic potion as you can get.

Thích Nhất Hạnh, peace activist

Exercising mindfully is an incredibly powerful stress reliever. When you're working out, be fully in the present moment. This is your time to focus completely on yourself. Bring awareness to your breath and the physical capabilities of your body. Feel every stretch deeply and commit to giving every move your all. When you focus on what you're doing, you improve the quality of your movement and, as a result, the quality of your overall workout. Feel your own strength and power as you exercise.

Exercising in this way is a very grounding experience and will help you to feel more connected with your mind and body. Over time you will find that your focus is increased and your overall mood is improved.

cleaning

If you clean the floor with love, you have given the world an invisible painting.

Osho, mystic

When cleaning your home, notice any feelings of resistance and urges to get it done as quickly as possible. Then focus on the doing, not the getting done. The motion of simple tasks can make you more attentive and calm – the back and forth of the vacuum cleaner, for example. Chores can be meditative, just so long as you're not thinking about how much you hate them. There is much comfort and peace to be found in repetitive tasks.

leaves in the stream meditation

Just as trees shed their leaves in winter and renew themselves,
the mind can shed its prejudices, barriers and renew itself.

*Radha Burnier, Seventh International President of the
Theosophical Society*

Whilst sitting quietly, bring your focus to your breath. Start
to notice the thoughts that come into your mind. As you
notice each thought, imagine putting those words on to
a leaf as it floats by on a stream. Place each thought that
you notice on to a leaf, and watch it drift on by. There's no
need to look for the thoughts, or to remain alert waiting
for them to come. Just let them come, and when they do,
place them on to a leaf.

let go of resentment

Resentment is like taking poison and waiting for the other person to die.

Malachy McCourt

If you have an ill feeling towards another, today is the day to let it go. Sit in a comfortable position and bring awareness to your breathing. Focus on inhaling warm, open thoughts and dispelling negative ones. Bring to mind the person you feel resentment towards and direct loving thoughts towards them. Say out loud, "I wish love, health, peace and happiness for (insert name)." Although this may feel awkward at first, the feelings of peace and love will eventually replace any negative ones.

Once you have fully let go of your anger and resentment, you will immediately feel lighter. You may even find that you feel more awake and rejuvenated now that you aren't wasting energy on toxic thoughts and feelings.

eat lunch outside

Being able to smell the fresh air and disconnect from the news and your phone – there's nothing like it.

Jason Ward, naturalist, birder and activist

Make the effort to eat lunch outside today. Savour each mouthful in your mindful eating, relish every flavour whilst enjoying the air in your lungs and the breeze against your skin. If you're unable to get out then at least try to sit near an open window.

Whilst you are eating your lunch, leave your phone behind, or if you are eating by a window, leave it somewhere where you won't be tempted to pick it up. This will help you to fully appreciate the sounds of nature and the smell of fresh air, and will help you to concentrate on the taste of your food, leaving you feeling fuller and more satisfied.

take a power snooze

Think what a better world it would be if we all, the whole world, had cookies and milk about three o'clock every afternoon and then lay down on our blankets for a nap.

Barbara Jordan, lawyer, educator, politician and activist

At some point today take 10 minutes out for a reviving catnap. Make yourself comfortable and bring awareness to your breathing. Notice any noise around you and let the sounds sink into the distant background. Feel yourself removed from them. Allow your body to become heavy, sinking into the chair or bed. Let your thoughts drift and your body relax entirely. If you manage to drop off, you will feel refreshed and revived on waking. (It is advisable to set a timer before you begin!) If you struggle to nod off whilst it's bright outside, try using an eyemask.

Studies have shown that a twenty minute rest with your eyes closed – even if you don't manage to fall asleep – can have huge benefits for your mind and body, improving focus and productivity.

write a stream of
consciousness journal

Rule your mind or it will rule you.

Buddha

This is something you could do either in the morning to clear your head in preparation for the day, or at bedtime to empty your mind of clutter before sleep. Set a timer for five minutes and in this time write down all of your tumbling thoughts. Whatever comes into your mind, write it down. Just relax your mind, let the thoughts come and your pen flow easily across the page.

Don't worry about whether or not what you have written makes sense; you don't even have to read it back if you don't want to. The most important thing is that you get your thoughts down on to a piece of paper and out of your head. In doing so, not only are you decluttering your mind, you are improving your understanding of your thoughts and feelings, and will gain a deeper understanding of your emotions and how they affect your day-to-day life.

the 50/10 rule

Everything we do is infused with the energy with which we do it. If we're frantic, life will be frantic. If we're peaceful, life will be peaceful.

Marianne Williamson, author and political activist

Today, for every 50 minutes you spend on a task, take 10 minutes out to refocus your mind.

It is incredibly important to make sure you are taking regular breaks during your day, especially whilst at work. Not only will this help to ease any feeling of stress and anxiety, it will also help to improve your focus and productivity. And coming back to a task with a rested and fresh pair of eyes will help you to complete it to an even better standard.

33

today's to-do list

Nothing can bring you peace but yourself.

Ralph Waldo Emerson, philosopher and abolitionist

inhale

exhale

inhale

exhale

inhale

exhale

34   inhale

exhale

track your daily
accomplishments

I believe in living today. Not in yesterday, nor in tomorrow.

Loretta Young, actress

As the day concludes, find yourself a quiet space and write a list of everything you have achieved today. Remember to think moments, not miracles.

As you may have already read earlier on in this book, it doesn't matter how small your daily achievements are. Whether it's doing the dishes, folding the laundry or cleaning the bathroom, every little thing counts!

mood surf

Change your thoughts and you change your world.

Norman Vincent Peale, minister and author

Throughout the day, check into your mood. Bring awareness to your breathing, then tap into how you are feeling. Angry? Tired? Frustrated? Bored? Whatever your mood, simply notice it, acknowledge it and then return to your task. This is a simple and effective way to break the cycle of unchecked negative moods.

It will also help you to gain a better understanding of your thoughts and emotions. If you find yourself in a particularly bad mood, ask yourself why that is. Are you frustrated because you are tired because you didn't get enough sleep? Are you distracted because you're hungry because you didn't eat a proper breakfast? Identifying the root cause of your moods will help you to strengthen the connection between your body and mind.

tune into your rhythm

I can't change the direction of the wind, but I can adjust my
sails to always reach my destination.

Jimmy Dean, singer and actor

Each of us has a natural rhythm. If you don't already know,
work out whether you're an early bird, a night owl, or
somewhere in between. When are you at your best? Instead
of trying to fight your body's natural rhythms, embrace
them and work them to your advantage.

You may find your natural rhythm fluctuates throughout
the day. Think particularly about when your highs and
lows are, and tailor your to-do list around them. Do you
tend to have a slump right after lunch? Are you better at
problem solving first thing in the morning? Make sure you
tune into exactly what your body is telling you and take the
time to adapt to its needs.

meditate on
difficult emotions

Peace of mind is not the absence of conflict from life, but the ability to cope with it.

Unknown

Find a quiet space to sit still and focus on your breathing. Let any negative thoughts and emotions you are experiencing wash over you, but instead of letting the thought or feeling overwhelm you, visualize it as a butterfly. Now watch the butterfly fluttering away from you.

It isn't always easy to meditate on difficult emotions, especially if you aren't used to making time to think about how you're feeling. At first, you may find it upsetting to think about the negative things in your life, but try to not let this put you off meditating on them. It's extremely important to work through your emotions rather than bottling them up. When you bottle your emotions up, they tend to build and build until they start to feel impossible to deal with. Take action before you get to this stage.

breathe

If you breathe in and are aware that you are alive – that you can touch the miracle of being alive – then that is a kind of enlightenment.

Thích Nhất Hạnh, peace activist

A simple breathing exercise for calming the overworked mind is a timed breath where the exhale is longer than the inhale. Set a timer for five minutes. Inhale for a count of two, hold the breath in for a count of one. Exhale gently, counting out to four and finish by holding the breath out for a count of one. You can alter the breath lengths to suit you, the most important thing is that the exhale is longer than the inhale. Keep your breathing even and smooth.

take a yoga class

Yoga practice can make us more and more sensitive to subtler and subtler sensations in the body. Paying attention to and staying with finer and finer sensations within the body is one of the surest ways to steady the wandering mind.

Ravir Avindra, author and professor

Yoga encourages you to relax, slow your breath, and focus on the present, shifting the balance from the sympathetic nervous system (or the fight-or-flight response) to the parasympathetic nervous system. The latter is calming and restorative; it can lower your breathing and heart rate as well as decreasing blood pressure.

I want to remember

The present moment is filled with joy and happiness. If you are attentive, you will see it.

Thích Nhất Hạnh, peace activist

Write an "I want to remember…" list. Choose little moments from today that you'd like to remember and note them down. This is a great way to ground you in what you love about your life.

Once you've been doing this for a while, it can be extremely rewarding to look back at all of your past memories. And when you have days where you aren't feeling your best, flicking through your memories from the past will help to soothe and put your current thoughts and feelings into perspective.

For a deeper and more significant experience, you can even purchase a special notebook to record your memories in.

eat mindfully

Today, when you eat your meals and snacks, eat mindfully. This approach involves bringing your full attention to the process of eating – to all the tastes, smells, thoughts and feelings that arise during a meal. Before you begin to eat, pause. Look at your food, inhale the scent. When you eat take small bites and chew slowly. Be fully present in the moment with your experience, savouring the tastes and textures one morsel at a time.

By eating mindfully you can reclaim the pleasure of food. You will also find that you feel fuller and more satisfied at the end of your meal.

Opting for healthier foods can also enhance your mindful eating experience. As you eat, think about the vitamins and nutrients you are consuming, and the incredible benefits they have on your mind and body.

a mindful shower

In the midst of movement and chaos, keep stillness
inside of you.

Deepak Chopra, author

Take a mindful shower this morning. Instead of the usual
rush, notice the temperature of the water, and the feel
of it in your hair, on your shoulders and running down
your legs. Notice the smell of the soap and shampoo, and
the sensation of them against your skin. Notice the water
droplets on the shower screen, the water dripping down
your body and the steam rising upwards. When thoughts
arise, acknowledge them, let them be, and bring your
attention back to the shower.

If you are able to, purchase a slightly more luxurious
shower gel or body wash for the days you need a little more
TLC. Scents such as lavender and bergamot will help to
soothe and relax.

tune into beauty

Pause and remember – if you take the time to look for beauty, you will find it. Open yourself to the beauty you have been missing right before you.

Jenni Young, author and motivational speaker

Take a moment to notice beauty around you. There's beauty in every home, street, office and in that person sitting opposite you at the table.

Beauty comes in many forms, so pick something you find beautiful – tune fully into it and simply enjoy and appreciate the moment. It could be a home-cooked meal, an old tree in a park, or the sound of children's laughter.

Noticing beauty in your surroundings will teach you to notice all the beautiful parts of yourself and your own life, and will help you to truly appreciate the everyday.

review your day

How we spend our days is of course how we spend our lives.

Annie Dillard, author

As your day concludes, spend a few mindful moments reviewing the day without judgement. Release whatever happened and file away the lessons learned. In this way, you will sleep more peacefully.

Make sure you aren't just packing away any negative experiences and burying your feelings deep down – that is not the point of this exercise. Take the time to properly reflect on your day and to appreciate everything you have learned.

45

stop

Wisdom comes with the ability to be still. Just look and just listen. No more is needed.

Eckhart Tolle, author and spiritual teacher

Try the STOP sign technique when responding to emails today:

S = Stop (do nothing)

T = Take a breath (or breathe until you're more relaxed)

O = Observe (What are you feeling and thinking?)

P = Proceed (when you feel calm again. Now you can respond if you need to)

go slow

Smile, breathe and go slowly.

Thích Nhất Hạnh, peace activist

You can do one task at a time, but also rush that task. Instead, take your time, and move slowly. Make your actions deliberate, not rushed and random. It takes practice, but it helps you focus on the task.

You may think you don't have the time to slow down, but doing this can actually make you more productive. If you rush through things, you increase your chances of making mistakes or missing important details, meaning you'll only end up having to go back and fix these issues, wasting more time in the process. Slow and steady wins the race – it's a cliché for a reason!

clouds in the sky meditation

If you surrender completely to the moments as they pass, you live more richly those moments.

Anne Morrow Lindbergh, author and aviator

When you notice a thought come into your mind, just put the thought on a cloud as it drifts across the sky or dissipates. No judgements. The thoughts and feelings aren't good or bad. They just are.

Putting your thoughts on clouds in this way will force you to take your time and slow your thinking, rather than just letting any random thought fly in and out of your mind. This will help you to identify your mind's most prevalent thoughts in the current moment, which will, in turn, further your understanding of your emotions for increased mindfulness.

let go of regrets

Life is too short to argue and fight with the past. Count your blessings, value your loved ones, and move on with your head held high.

Unknown

Today, make the positive life decision to let go of any regrets. Take 10 minutes out of your day to sit somewhere quiet and comfortable. Bring awareness to your breathing and reflect on any regrets you have, without letting them overwhelm you. See them as separate from your self. Now visualize these regrets floating away like balloons into the sky.

Once you have practised doing this, you'll find negative thoughts don't stick around as long as they used to. You'll realize there is more to life than dwelling on the past, and will be able to free up your mind in order to live more fully in the present.

do less

It's surprising how much free time and productivity you gain
when you lose the busyness in your mind.

Brittany Burgunder, eating disorder and life coach

If you do less, you can do those things more slowly, more
completely and with more concentration. If you fill your
day with tasks, you will be rushing from one thing to the
next without stopping to think about what you do. It's a
matter of working out what's important, and letting go of
what's not.

Reframing your day-to-day in this way will help you to see
the bigger picture and will give your life more meaning
and purpose.

be kind to yourself

You can't calm the storm... so stop trying. What you can do is
calm yourself. The storm will pass.

Timber Hawkeye, author

Today treat yourself to something you love – maybe
indulge in your favourite food, read a good book in
the bath, take a walk in a place you love, go dancing
... Whatever you choose to do, be fully present in the
wonderful moment in which you have rewarded yourself.

It's extremely important to determine exactly what being
kind to yourself means to you. When you're having a bad
day, tune into what your body is telling you. Do your
muscles feel stiff or sore? Treat yourself to a long bath. Are
you feeling especially tired and worn out? Treat yourself to
an extra hour in bed.

recognize the good in others

Those who are free of resentful thoughts surely find peace.

Buddha

Today, project a positive spin on all your relationships and encounters. Look for the best in everyone you interact with. For every negative thought you associate with a person, think of something positive about them. In this way, you are inviting positivity into your own life.

cook mindfully

If you truly get in touch with a piece of carrot, you get in touch with the soil, the rain, the sunshine. You get in touch with Mother Earth and eating in such a way, you feel in touch with true life, your roots, and that is meditation.

Thích Nhất Hạnh, peace activist

Cooking provides a wonderful opportunity to be present, mindful and aware. As you prepare your food, notice the colours and textures. As your food cooks, listens to the sounds it makes – maybe oil sizzling, or water bubbling. Notice the smells that arise from each ingredient. Absorb these aromas. Try to recognize the smell of each ingredient in the dish. As your mind wanders, gently bring it back to your senses, to the sounds and smells of your cooking.

queue mindfully

Without patience, we will learn less in life. We will see less.

Mother Teresa, nun and missionary

This is about finding a moment of stillness amongst chaos. If you find yourself having to queue today, acknowledge the feelings of frustration or anger that may arise, but then bring awareness to your breathing; follow the course of the in-breath, all the way in and then the out-breath, all the way out. Take a moment to explore the sights around you and focus on something pleasant that you can see. Take a moment to savour this.

You'll find that in queuing mindfully, you won't be left feeling as though you've wasted your time standing in line when you hadn't planned to.

go outside

Look deep into nature, and then you will understand everything better.

Albert Einstein, theoretical physicist

Being outdoors can relieve stress, while also improving energy levels, memory and attention. Even if you can only manage to get out for five minutes, it will give you a vital mental reboot.

The Japanese practice of Shinrin Yoku – or forest bathing – involves going for walks or taking breaks in the forest. It has been heavily associated with improved mental well-being, and, recently, medical professionals have started to recommend it to their patients.

If you aren't able to go for a walk in a forest or wooded area, try and find a park or any green spot where you can get some air and appreciate nature.

apply a filter to your life

Your mind is a flexible mirror, adjust it to see a better world.

Amit Ray, author and spiritual teacher

In other words, filter out all that is unnecessary. Sit quietly and bring awareness to your breathing. Visualize sand streaming through a sieve. The sand represents the flow of your life. Once all the sand has filtered through, you are left with a pile of stones that won't fit through the small holes in the sieve. These stones represent the thoughts, feelings, people or objects that form some kind of obstacle in your life. Name these stones for what they are – one may be financial worries, another a friend who makes you feel bad… Then visualize throwing these stones into the sea and feel your unnecessary baggage sinking with them.

self-esteem mantras

The happiness of your life depends upon the quality
of your thoughts.

Marcus Aurelius, philosopher

Today bring the following mantras to mind whenever your
confidence needs a boost:

'I am worth it.'

'I can do it.'

'I know who I am and I am enough.'

It's surprisingly easy to "trick" your mind into believing
what you are telling it, so the more you recite these positive
mantras, the more you will start to truly believe that
anything is possible.

mind mapping

A calm mind is a clear mind.

Veronica Roth

Mind mapping is a technique that creates visuals of your thoughts and helps unclutter your mind to bring focus and clarity. You can indulge in this cathartic process today by downloading a mind mapping app, or look for artistic inspiration online if you'd prefer to create your own visual masterpiece.

Bullet journalling is also a great way of organizing your thoughts on paper, and is also excellent for boosting creativity. Treat yourself to a special notebook and some coloured pens for a more rewarding experience.

one-minute exercise

Miracles come in moments. Be ready and willing.

Wayne Dyer, author and motivational speaker

Sit in front of a clock or watch that you can use to time the passing of one minute. Your task is to focus your entire attention on your breathing, and nothing else, for the minute. Leave your eyes open and breathe normally. Be ready to catch your mind from wandering off (because it will) and return your attention to your breath whenever it does so.

slow down your thoughts

Restore your attention or bring it to a new level by
dramatically slowing down whatever you're doing.

Sharon Salzberg, author and meditation teacher

Find somewhere quiet and comfortable to sit. Bring
awareness to your breathing and "watch" the flitting
thoughts as they race through your mind. Focus on your
breathing. Check back in with your thoughts. Have they
slowed a little? Keep going back to focus on your breathing
until your thoughts have slowed or are still. This could take
5 minutes, 25 minutes or more.

Be patient, and don't beat yourself up if at first you
struggle to calm your thoughts. The more you practise, the
quicker you will find you are able to reach a place of calm.

spend time alone

We need solitude, because when we're alone, we're free from obligations, we don't need to put on a show, and we can hear our own thoughts.

Tamim Ansary, author

Try and spend some of today completely alone. Spending time on your own brings peace and nourishment to the soul. It can slow down your thoughts and make you feel more grounded in the present.

Spending time alone is also a really great way of getting to know yourself and becoming more in-tune with your thoughts and emotions. Pay attention to how you're feeling. If you aren't feeling particularly great, now is the time to discover that only you – and you alone – can truly make yourself feel better. Think about what you can do to pick yourself up and go ahead and do them, whether it's a walk in the park or fixing yourself up a special meal.

say a selective yes

Somedays you just have to create your own sunshine.

Unknown

Today only say "yes" to people and situations that support your well-being.

Do your best to not feel pressured into doing things you don't want to do. Life is far too short to waste time on doing anything that doesn't truly bring you joy.

banish negativity

Your experience of life isn't based on your life, but on what you pay attention to.

Gregg Krech, author and poet

Use a negative thought arising as a prompt to be mindful. When you recognize that you having such a thought, simply label it as negative. Visualize it written on a piece of paper. Now scrunch it up and throw it in the bin. Now visualise being left with a completely blank piece of paper. Mentally write a positive thought on that page to replace the negative one you have just discarded.

Though completely banishing negativity isn't always easy, the above will inspire you to see things in a different way. And with practice, you'll find it comes easily – you won't have to act out the process of throwing your negative thoughts into the bin, as you will have shifted your mindset so that it happens naturally.

decrease your distractions

You are the sky. Everything else is just the weather.

Pema C. Hödrön, author and nun

Today, pledge to decrease your distractions. Limit the time you spend watching television, don't respond to texts that aren't urgent, silence your phone for a while (or better yet, turn it off). If you find you aren't able to keep this up for a whole day, aim for at least an hour or so around the most important times of the day, such as mealtimes and sleep.

Limiting your distractions will help you to focus on the task at hand and will also help to improve your ability to concentrate on the here and now.

find your happy place

If you correct your mind, the rest of your life will
fall into place.

Lao Tzu, philosopher and writer

To find your happy place think about who or what makes
you incredibly happy. Your family? Friends? Travelling? A
hobby you're passionate about? Walking beside the sea?
Solitude or socializing?

Take a moment to picture whatever or whoever makes you
happy. Close your eyes, clear your mind and go to your
happy place. What do you feel, hear, smell? Spend a few
minutes there. Whenever the day gets tough, or you just
need some time out, tune in to your happy place again.

You may find it helps to write down the details of your
happy place for next time. In doing so, you'll be able to
transport yourself there that much quicker in the future.

look out of the window

When we recognize the virtues, the talent, the beauty
of Mother Earth, something is born in us, some kind of
connection, love is born.

Thích Nhất Hạnh, peace activist

When we are busy indoors we seem to forget that we are
part of the world outside. If you are working inside today,
make the effort to look out of the window, even if only for
a short while. This works particularly well if there is some
nature outside to focus on – trees, flowers, birds or simply
the clouds in the sky are all useful focal points to bring us
back into the present moment. If it's warm out, leave the
window open to allow fresh air in.

Being near a window will also give you the much-needed
sunlight your body needs for its natural rhythms, and will
help to boost your mood and overall well-being.

prepare for a good night's sleep

We humans have lost the wisdom of genuinely resting and relaxing. We worry too much. We don't allow our bodies to heal, and we don't allow our minds and hearts to heal.

Thích Nhất Hạnh, peace activist

As you lie in bed tonight, bring awareness to your breathing for a few minutes. Then start to focus on a body part. As you focus on it clench the muscle and relax it, then move on to the next, working your way around the body. As your brain travels up your body, stop in each place to repeat the muscle clenching and relaxing. If your mind wanders, just gently bring it back to the body part.

It goes without saying these days that spending time on your phone before sleep is never a good idea; it only serves to fill your head with more unwanted clutter. If you find it really difficult to not look at your phone during bedtime, start by reducing the amount of time you spend on it. Start with one night, increase it to two and then go from there.

leave no trace

How freeing a thought: instead of worrying about
leaving a legacy, to leave no trace of one's existence.
How liberating indeed!

Kamand Kojouri, author, poet and educator

This is an exercise to increase awareness of the impact you
have on your environment. The aim is to leave whatever
room you have been in exactly the same, as if you had
never been there. So, for example, if you are making
dinner in the kitchen, clean up as you go along. If you have
finished with your coffee cup, wash it up and put it away.
Wipe up any spills you have made. Pick up anything you
drop, and so on.

By doing this, we are drawing away from our hurried
nature, mindfully taking care of the little things that take
care of us.

listen

Let go of your mind and then be mindful. Close your
ears and listen!

Rumi, poet and scholar

We often confuse hearing for listening. Hearing is just
perceiving the sounds around you. You can hear someone
while typing a text message, for example. Listening is
the intentional choice to fully pay attention to the other
person – from the tone and texture of their voice to their
emotional state and body language.

Today, when you ask your loved one how their day was, for
example, be sure to really listen. Take in what they're saying
without projecting what you feel or expect on to their
words. Don't think of your reply as they are speaking; wait
until they are finished. Take time to think about how you
want to respond before doing so.

write a letter

Today, write a letter to somebody you care about. Feel grounded and present as you write, and content in the knowledge that you are sharing this moment with someone who is important to you.

Writing a message on pen and paper may feel old fashioned, but it will help you to really think about what you are saying, allowing you to express yourself more truthfully and thoughtfully.

Writing a letter can be especially therapeutic if the subject is a tough or sensitive one. By writing it down on pen and paper, you are getting it out of your system. And you don't have to send the letter if you end up changing your mind.

be grateful

There's a lot that is good in your life – don't take it for granted. Don't get so focused on the struggles that you miss the gift of today.

Joel Osteen, author and pastor

Create a mental list of things in your life for which you are grateful – even better, write them down.

Studies have shown that writing down just three good things from your day can do wonders for improving your mental well-being.

mindful washing up

You must learn a new way to think before you can master a
new way to be.

Marianne Williamson, author and spiritual leader

Any mundane household task can be transformed into a
mindful meditation. Simply by grounding yourself in the
moment and completing each task slowly and intentionally,
you can bring a sense of calm to the proceedings.

Wash one item at a time and focus on what you're doing.
What does the water feel like on your hands? What does
the water sound like as you begin washing up? The smell
of the washing up liquid, the play of the light on the
water, the feel of the cloth against the plate ... If your mind
wanders, simply bring it back to the task in hand.

take a walk

You can make any human activity into meditation simply by
being completely with it and doing it just to do it.

Alan W. Watts, philosopher

Solvitur ambulando is Latin for "it is solved by walking."
Today, go for a walk, preferably somewhere away from the
crowds. It is an excellent way to calm the mind, gain new
perspective and facilitate greater awareness. The fresh air
will also help to rejuvenate and boost your energy. Aim for
20 to 30 minutes a day.

Taking a walk through a park or quiet green spot is most
beneficial, but if you aren't able to find a quiet place to go,
put your headphones on and listen to music that helps to
calm and soothe you.

focus on nature

Our goal should be to live life in radical amazement ... get up in the morning and look at the world in a way that takes nothing for granted. Everything is phenomenal – everything is incredible – never treat life casually.

Abraham Joshua Heschel, rabbi and theologian

Pick a natural organism within your immediate environment and focus on watching it for a minute or two. This could be a leaf or an insect, the clouds or the moon. Don't do anything except notice the thing you are looking at. But really notice it. Look at it as if you are seeing it for the first time. Visually explore every aspect of this glorious element of the natural world. Allow your spirit to connect with its role and purpose in the world. Allow yourself just to notice and "be".

74

end the day on
a positive note

There is nothing either good or bad but thinking makes it so.

William Shakespeare, playwright

Write down three positive things that have happened
to you today. This will help you recognize that good
things have happened, however small, and will keep you
grounded in the best aspects of your life.

As you will have already read earlier on in this book, it
doesn't matter how small the positive moment is. The most
important thing is that it made you feel good.

75

accept your feelings

If it comes, let it come. If it goes, it's okay, let it go. Let things come and go. Stay calm, don't let anything disturb your peace, and carry on.

Germany Kent, journalist

If something is causing you distress or making you angry, however it is disrupting your inner calm, don't avoid the emotion. Try to get in touch with the feelings, not in a confrontational way but rather just to acknowledge and accept them.

Note that the emotion is transient and will pass, no matter how hard things may seem at the time.

76

retain perspective

Serenity comes when you trade expectations for acceptance.

Buddha

Don't add unnecessary stress to everyday ordeals, most of which are trivial. Unless it's a life-or-death situation, remind yourself that it really doesn't matter that much.

This is the case in all areas of your life, whether you've missed a deadline at work, haven't been to the gym in weeks, or whether the laundry is piling up or you just can't face doing the dishes. Let it go; try again tomorrow.

When you put these annoying "failures" in life into perspective, you'll soon come to realize that spending time worrying about them is in fact a complete waste of time.

don't over-schedule

Savour a slow-paced contented life.

Fennel Hudson, author, broadcaster and publisher

Inner peace can only be achieved when you're fully present in the moment. Over-stretching yourself means you will spend every day frantic and preoccupied, worried about the next place you have to be and the next thing you need to be doing.

Keep your to-do list to the most vital tasks that need doing urgently; anything else can wait. When you have less to think about, you'll be able to concentrate more fully on these vital tasks, meaning you'll probably get through them more quickly.

visualize

Meditation is such a wonderful way to calm the ocean inside us.

Debasish Mridha, M.D., physician and philosopher

A visualizing meditation can be wonderful way to cultivate calm:

1. Close your eyes and imagine yourself in a comforting place where you can fully relax.

2. Really notice how it feels in this safe place. What can you see? What can you hear? What you can smell?

3. Stay in your calm place for a while until you are ready to open your eyes.

4. Reflect on how this meditation has made you feel.

Bring to mind this visualization to recapture this feeling of serenity whenever you need to find peace.

create a zen zone

Breathe in deeply to bring your mind home to your body.

Thích Nhất Hạnh, peace activist

Set up a haven of calm in a cozy corner of your house. It could be a corner of your living room or a spare room in the house. If you're feeling ambitious, you could even convert an outdoor space like a garden shed. Just make sure it's a place away from noise and distractions.

A favourite chair, soft cushions, and low lighting or candles should feature. Take yourself there whenever you need to find a moment of peace.

As you may have read earlier on in this book, pay attention to the colours you decide to fill your zen space with. Try to include soft pastel colours to promote a sense of calm and tranquillity – darker, bold colours can sometimes cause tension and uneasiness.

practise compassion

Compassion is the ultimate expression of your highest self.

Russell Simmons

Inner peace is difficult to attain if you are constantly focused on yourself and your own worries. When you make the time to care for others you become a more positive and peaceful person.

The next time you find yourself judging someone, or jumping to conclusions about them, take the time to truly listen to and understand them. The more you practice compassion for others, the more you will find you can have compassion for yourself.

81

worry less

Happy is the person who can keep a quiet heart, in the chaos
and tumult of this modern world.

Patience Strong, poet

Worrying won't change the outcome of any event, but it
will take away your peace of mind today. Each time you
find yourself worrying about something, try to replace that
worry with a positive thought about that person or event.
This will help you to remain mindful throughout the day.

tune in

Eat, sleep, eat. Exist slowly, softly, like these trees, like a puddle of water.

Jean-Paul Sartre, philosopher and writer

Choose a day to rise with the sun, eat when you're hungry, drink when you're thirsty, and sleep when you're tired. You'll probably find that your body's needs tend to fluctuate depending on your daily activities, so make sure you really pay attention to your needs.

This can be a wonderful way of tuning in to your body's natural rhythms and finding an inner calm that is hard to attain within the usual daily structure of alarm clocks and deadlines. Becoming more mindful of what your body is telling you it wants will leave you feeling more fulfilled and satisfied, and is a great way of strengthening the connection between your body and mind.

83

see the bigger picture

Rule number one is, don't sweat the small stuff. Rule number two is, it's all small stuff.

Robert Eliot, writer

When we're stressed or frustrated it's often because we are unable to step out from our own limited viewpoint and see the bigger picture – to understand where others are coming from and put it all in perspective. Try to step outside of yourself today and take a bird's-eye view of any stressful situation. Gaining true perspective is incredibly calming.

For example, say you are on a packed rush-hour train and you start to feel anxious. Imagine seeing yourself from a bird's-eye view and state, to yourself and in your head, your situation in simple terms without over-analysing it. You'd probably say something incredibly simple like "I am on a train, headed home after work." Doing this puts your situation into perspective and helps to remove anxiety and stress.

tie up loose ends

If you want to fly, give up everything that weighs you down.

Unknown

Leave nothing unresolved in your life and inner peace will be far easier to achieve. Regret the way you left things with an old friend? Get in touch and tell them as much. Maybe you have an argument hanging over your head? Call the person you've argued with and talk it through.

This also applies to the smaller parts of life. For example, if you have an important email to send off, don't wait till the following morning to do it. Send it off now so you aren't left worrying about it overnight. This will help you to truly switch off and give your mind a break.

notice your reaction

The time to relax is when you don't have time for it.

Sydney J. Harris, journalist

Focus on your senses when you're feeling wound up or stressed. Notice how your palms are sweaty, or your heart is beating faster. Perhaps your breathing has become shallower or you're starting to fidget.

Don't judge these reactions, just calmly acknowledge them and your body will switch out of its automatic stress response far more quickly. Over time and with practice, you'll find that when stress and anxiety start to rear their ugly heads, you'll be able to deal with it in just a few short moments, leaving you free to get on with your day.

does it matter?

Sometimes people let the same problem make them miserable
for years when they could just say, 'So what.' That's one of my
favourite things to say. 'So what.'

Andy Warhol, artist

When you next find yourself stressing over an issue, ask
yourself will this matter next week, next month, next year,
in five years…? The answer, more often than not, will be a
resounding no.

move your body

It is easy to have calmness in inactivity, it is hard to have calmness in activity, but calmness in activity is true calmness.

Shunryū Suzuki, monk and teacher

Exercise releases feel-good endorphins, helps to balance stress hormones, and is an essential component of our overall well-being. Even if you can't fit in regular vigorous workouts, take the stairs instead of the elevator, park further away and walk the last block, dance while you're waiting for the kettle to boil.

It's essential that you don't adopt an all-or-nothing approach to exercise – make sure to move as much as you can. A few minutes a day is far better than doing nothing at all.

choose calm

By staying calm, you increase your resistance against any kind of storm.

Mehmet Murat İldan, writer

You alone are responsible for your own reactions to any situation. You can choose your behaviour at any given moment. Mentally prepare yourself for difficult situations and envisage your calm and measured response.

Remember to keep in mind the other techniques used in this book such as being mindful of perspective, seeing the bigger picture, and practising compassion. When you always have these at the back of your mind, you'll find it much easier to choose to be calm in stressful situations.

count to 10

Raise your words, not your voice. It is rain that grows flowers, not thunder.

Rumi, poet and scholar

Feel the rage brewing, tears prickling the backs of your eyes? Try the old-tech method of counting to 10. Distancing yourself from the situation at hand for this short time will allow you to drop back in with a refreshed, calmer mind.

know yourself

When you find peace within yourself, you become the kind of person who can live at peace with others.

Peace Pilgrim, spiritual teacher

Inner peace will only come with knowledge of your authentic self. Take time to meditate on your values, your passions, your goals ... and anything else that defines you as a unique individual.

Getting to know yourself is essential for maintaining mindfulness in your day-to-day life. Only by knowing yourself can you seek out the things that bring you true joy and leave you feeling content and fulfilled.

Don't feel bad if at first you find it difficult to make a list of your values and goals. Taking the time to really think about it and being honest with yourself is an important part of the process.

cleanse your life

There's calm in the mind of the humble. An unmistakable peace of not having to prove anything to anyone.

Ron Baratono, writer and actor

Keep your life as simple and honest as possible. Let go of all the people and extraneous material goods that no longer serve you.

There are several ways you can begin to cleanse your life, some of which have already been mentioned in this book. Decluttering your home is a great place to start, as is learning to practise mindful communication with the people that mean the most to you. Once you start, you'll find that unnecessary items are easy to get rid of, and that the people who aren't true friends will start to fall away, leaving you free to focus on the parts of your life that really matter.

escape

Relaxation comes from letting go of tense thoughts.

Frances Wilshire, author

You don't need to run for the hills to do this. Simply reading a good book or watching a favourite movie will allow you to relax and escape to another world free from the pressures of everyday life.

You can also experience escapism during exercise – put your headphones in and go for a run or a long walk. Or if you're in need of something more relaxing, put some gentle music on, light some candles and run yourself a bath, taking the time to pamper yourself. Concentrate on what makes you feel good and you'll forget all about the bad parts of your day.

93

breathe from your diaphragm

Peace begins from within, if you are not peaceful inside, the world will be chaotic.

Unknown

When anxious or stressed our breathing tends to be quick and shallow. Combat this by breathing deeply into your diaphragm. Check your breathing by placing one hand on your chest and the other on your lower abdomen. As you inhale, you should feel your belly rise.

When you're feeling particularly anxious, you'll find it helps to breathe in through your nose and out through your mouth, and to also exhale for longer than you inhale. This is because an excess of oxygen in your body – caused by rapid and shallow breathing – can lead to the unpleasant physical side effects of anxiety, such as light headedness and tingling in the fingers.

forgive

Forgiveness is not an occasional act; it is a constant attitude.

Martin Luther King, Jr.

Forgive yourself first and then you will find it easier to forgive others. You cannot achieve inner peace if you are harbouring resentments. When you forgive, you set yourself free from negative thought patterns that impede your ability to find peace.

When you practise forgiveness, you will experience feelings of lightness and may even find your energy levels increase. This is because you will no longer be wasting time on toxic thoughts and feelings.

let go of the need to be liked by everyone

Not caring more about what other people think than what you think. That's freedom.

Demi Moore, actress

When you focus too much on making people like you, you will lose sight of your authentic self. Stop being a people-pleaser and accept that you will never be everyone's favourite person.

Be true to yourself and your values, say no when you need to, and don't let anyone make you feel guilty for it. It may be hard to do at first, but with practice you will find it makes for a much happier life.